Meet the Math Facts™

Addition Level 1 Coloring Book

Preschool Prep® COMPANY

You will be amazed at what your little one can learn!™

866-451-5600
www.preschoolprepco.com
P.O. Box 1159, Danville CA 94526

2 + 2 = 4

1 + 4 = 5

2 + 3 = 5

1 + 6 = 7

3 + 5 = 8

$$1+0=1 \qquad 6+0=6$$

$$2+0=2 \qquad 7+0=7$$

$$3+0=3 \qquad 8+0=8$$

$$4+0=4 \qquad 9+0=9$$

$$5+0=5 \qquad 10+0=10$$